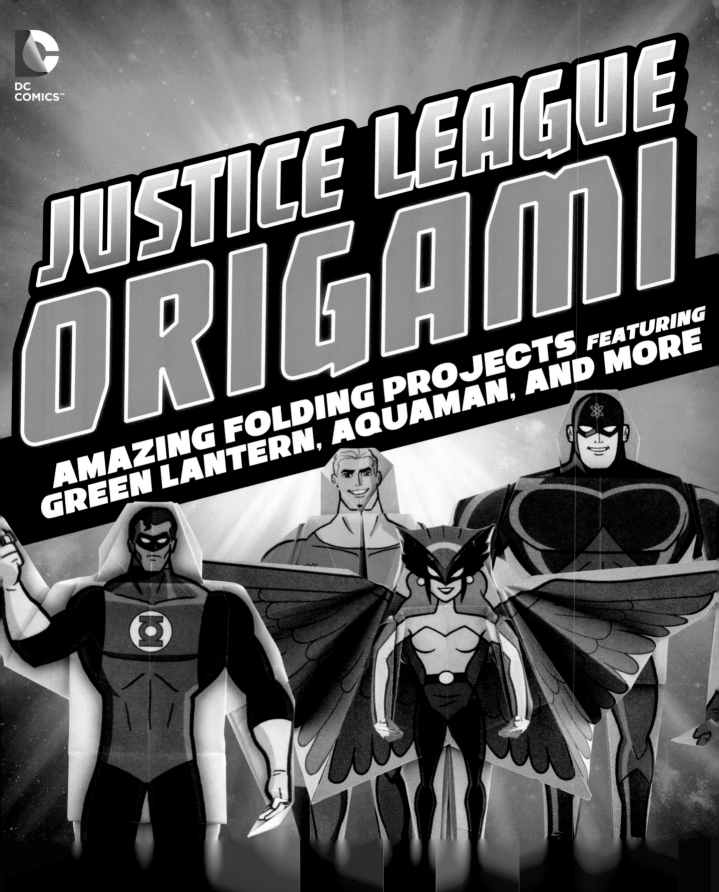

Published by Capstone Press in 2015
A Capstone Imprint
1710 Roe Crest Drive
North Mankato, Minnesota 56003
www.capstonepub.com

Library of Congress Cataloging-in-Publication Data
Montroll, John, author.
  Justice League origami : amazing folding projects featuring
Green Lantern, Aquaman, and more / by John Montroll.
      pages cm.—(DC super heroes. DC origami)
  Summary: "Provides instructions and diagrams for folding
origami models of characters, objects, and symbols related to
the Justice League"—Provided by publisher.
  Audience: Age 8–12.
  Audience: Grades 4–6.
  Includes bibliographical references.
  ISBN 978-1-4914-1789-8 (library binding)
  ISBN 978-1-4914-7596-6 (eBook PDF)
1. Origami—Juvenile literature. 2. Justice League of America
(Fictitious characters)—Juvenile literature. 3. Superheroes in
art—Juvenile literature. 4. Handicraft—Juvenile literature.
I. Title.
  TT872.5.M654 2015
    736.982—dc23   2015003764

Editorial Credits

Editor and Model Folder: Christopher Harbo
Designer: Lori Bye
Art Directors: Bob Lentz and Nathan Gassman
Contributing Writers: Donald Lemke and Michael Dahl
Folding Paper Illustrator: Min Sung Ku
Production Specialist: Kathy McColley

Photo Credits

Capstone Studio/Karon Dubke, all photos

Printed in the United States of America in North Mankato, MN.
052015 008823CGF15

TABLE OF CONTENTS

ORIGAMI JUSTICE 4
SYMBOLS 6   BASIC FOLDS 7

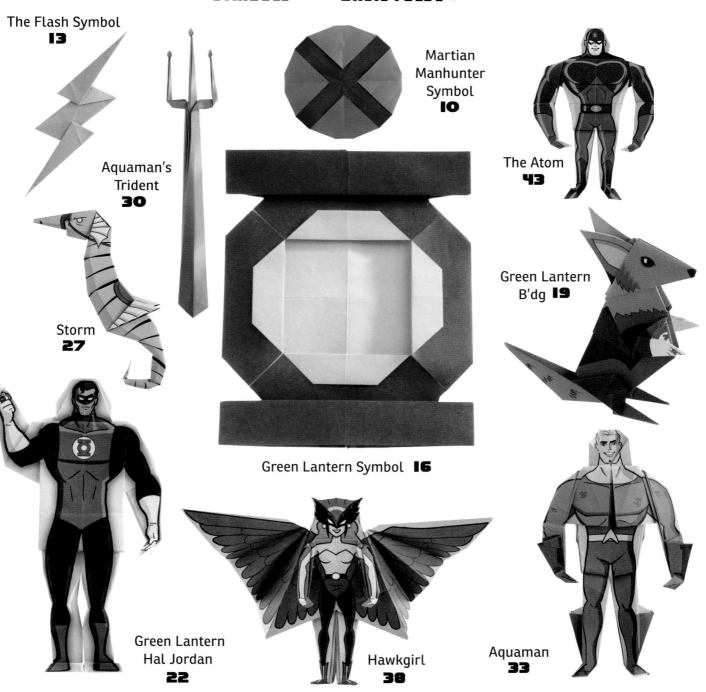

ORIGAMI JUSTICE

When the forces of evil grow stronger than one super hero can handle, the Justice League stands ready to join the fight. Led by Superman, Batman, and Wonder Woman, this team draws its strength from a powerful mix of crime fighters. Through the years, Aquaman, Green Lantern, The Flash, Martian Manhunter, The Atom, and many more have joined forces to vanquish the world's most dangerous super-villains. But never before has "joining the fold" of this super hero team been accomplished with a fold.

With the power of paper folding, the most remarkable collection of origami models ever created for the Justice League is now at your fingertips. From classic symbols for The Flash and Green Lantern to stunning figures for Aquaman and Hawkgirl, this collection has models everyone can enjoy. And once you've folded paper versions of Green Lantern B'dg and Aquaman's trusty steed, Storm, everyone you know will want one too!

No matter how much origami experience you've had, this book will help you succeed. The folding diagrams are drawn in the internationally approved Randlett-Yoshizawa style. This style is easy to follow once you learn the basic folds outlined in the pages to come. The models are also ranked to help you understand their level of difficulty. Simple models have one star, intermediate models have two stars, and the most complex models have three stars. Just remember, working through the collection from simplest to most complex is the best way to build your origami skills.

So don't wait another moment! Choose your favorite project, grab a square of paper, and behold the power of origami justice!

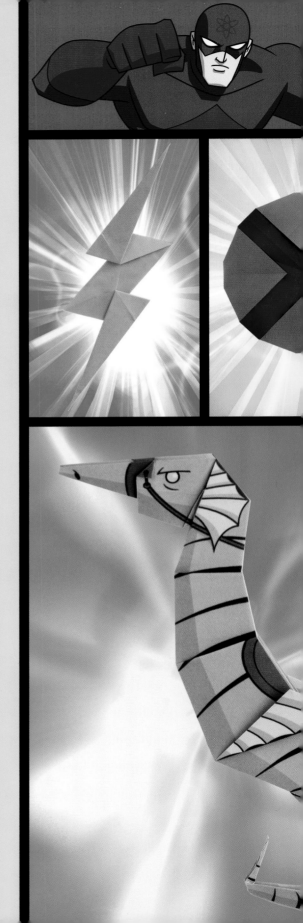

Symbols

Lines

— — — — — — — —   Valley fold, fold in front.

—··—··—··—··—··—   Mountain fold, fold behind.

————————————   Crease line.

····················   X-ray or guide line.

Arrows

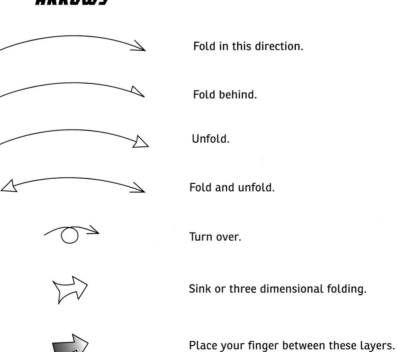

Fold in this direction.

Fold behind.

Unfold.

Fold and unfold.

Turn over.

Sink or three dimensional folding.

Place your finger between these layers.

Basic Folds

Pleat Fold

Fold back and forth. Each pleat is composed of one valley and mountain fold. Here are two examples.

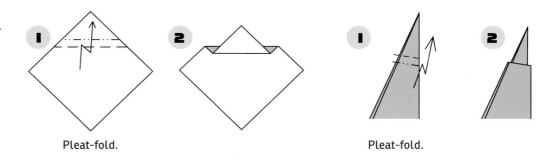

Pleat-fold.

Pleat-fold.

Squash Fold

In a squash fold, some paper is opened and then made flat. The shaded arrow shows where to place your finger.

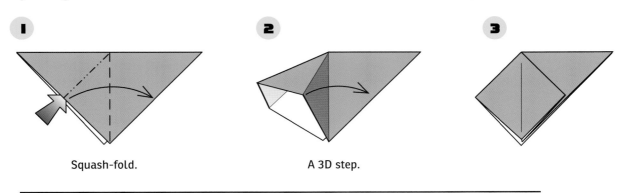

Squash-fold.

A 3D step.

Inside Reverse Fold

In an inside reverse fold, some paper is folded between layers. The inside reverse fold is generally referred to as a reverse fold. Here are two examples.

Reverse-fold.

Reverse-fold.

CRIMP FOLD

A crimp fold is a combination of two reverse folds. Open the model slightly to form the crimp evenly on each side. Here are two examples.

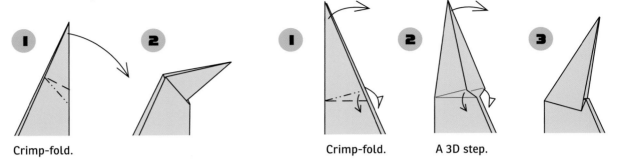

Crimp-fold.

Crimp-fold.   A 3D step.

OUTSIDE REVERSE FOLD

Much of the paper must be unfolded to wrap around, in order to make an outside reverse fold.

Outside-reverse-fold.

PETAL FOLD

In a petal fold, one point is folded up while two opposite sides meet each other.

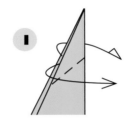

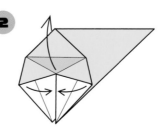

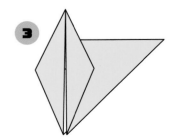

Petal-fold.   A 3D step.

8

Rabbit Ear

To fold a rabbit ear, one corner is folded in half and laid down to a side.

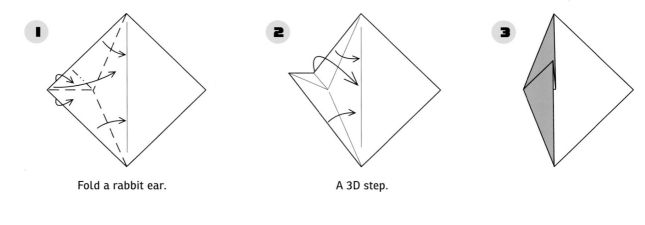

Fold a rabbit ear.

A 3D step.

Preliminary Fold

The preliminary fold is the starting point for many models. The maneuver in step 3 occurs in many other models.

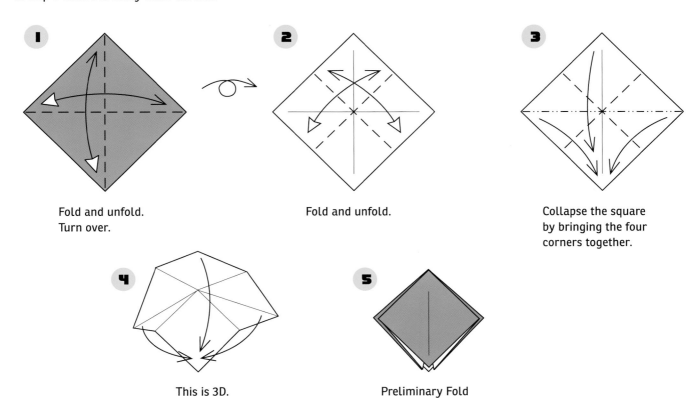

Fold and unfold.
Turn over.

Fold and unfold.

Collapse the square by bringing the four corners together.

This is 3D.

Preliminary Fold

MARTIAN MANHUNTER SYMBOL

J'onn J'onnz, the green-skinned hero from Mars, possesses the powers of his pal Superman and the detecting dexterity of Batman. To fight crime across his adopted planet, Earth, the Martian Manhunter unleashes his unearthly strength and super-breath. He also possesses abilities such as flight, invisibility, and shape-shifting—frequently assuming the human identity of police detective John Jones. Whenever he morphs into his true form, the Manhunter's blazing scarlet harness reminds bad guys that the Martian is an X-pert at crossing paths with criminals.

LEVEL: ★☆☆

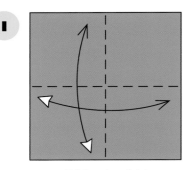

1

Fold and unfold.

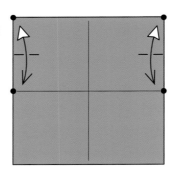

2

Fold and unfold on the edges.

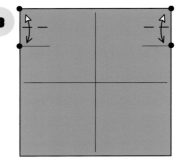

3

Fold and unfold on the edges.

4

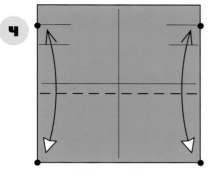

Fold and unfold.

5

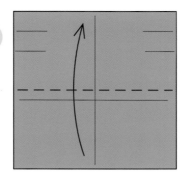

Fold in half.

6

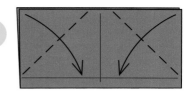

Fold the top layer down to the crease.

7

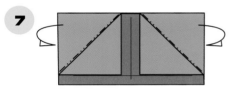

Fold behind.

8

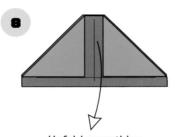

Unfold everything.

9

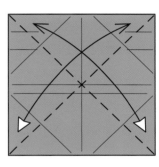

Fold and unfold.

10

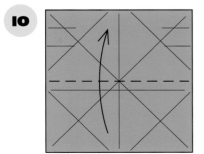

Fold along the crease.

11

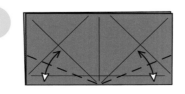

Fold and unfold.

12

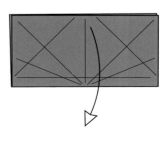

Unfold and rotate model 90°.

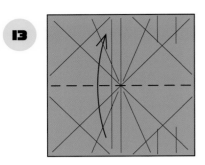

Repeat steps 10–12.

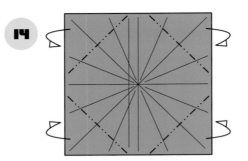

Fold along the creases.

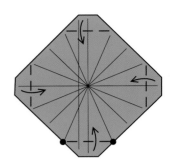

Fold four sides.

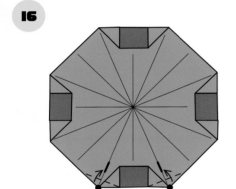

Fold the corners up
and rotate model 90°.

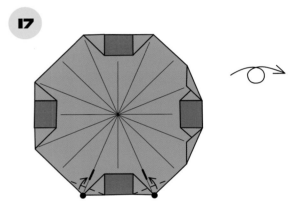

Repeat step 16 three times.
Rotate model and turn over.

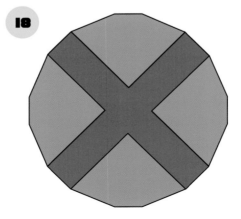

Martian Manhunter Symbol

THE FLASH SYMBOL

Emblazoned on The Flash's red-and-yellow uniform, the lightning bolt represents this super hero's amazing speed and incredible origin story. One stormy night, a bolt of lightning illuminated the laboratory of Barry Allen. It struck a case of dangerous chemicals, spilling them onto the police scientist and transforming him into the Scarlet Speedster. As the Fastest Man Alive, The Flash quickly handles Central City's worst criminals, known as the Rogues.

LEVEL: ★★☆

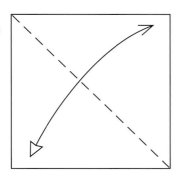

1 Fold and unfold.

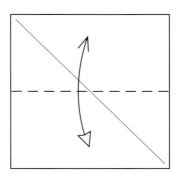

2 Fold and unfold.

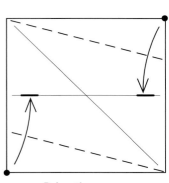

3 Bring the corners to the lines.

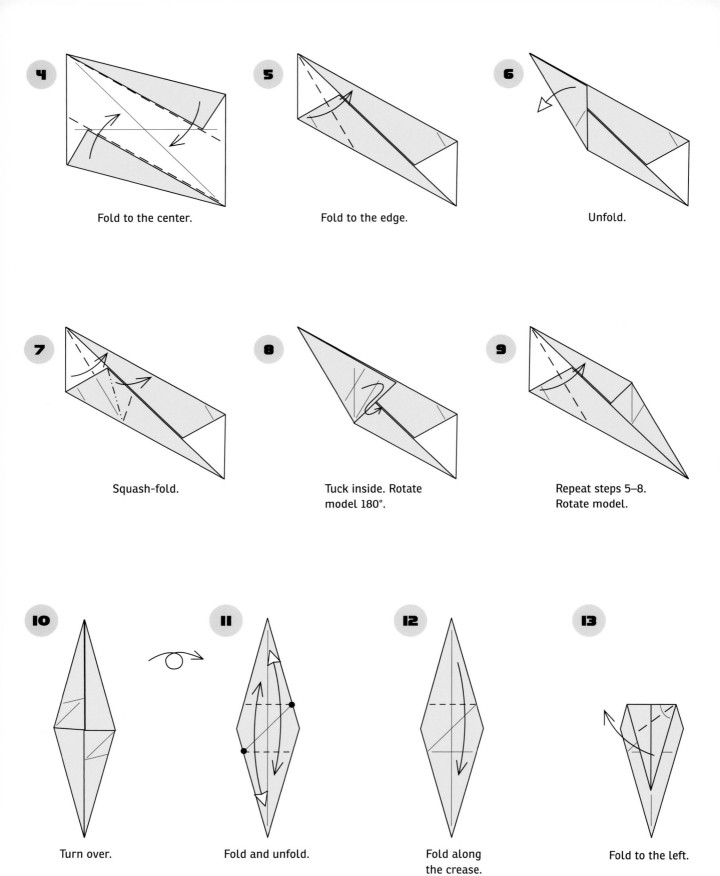

4 Fold to the center.

5 Fold to the edge.

6 Unfold.

7 Squash-fold.

8 Tuck inside. Rotate model 180°.

9 Repeat steps 5–8. Rotate model.

10 Turn over.

11 Fold and unfold.

12 Fold along the crease.

13 Fold to the left.

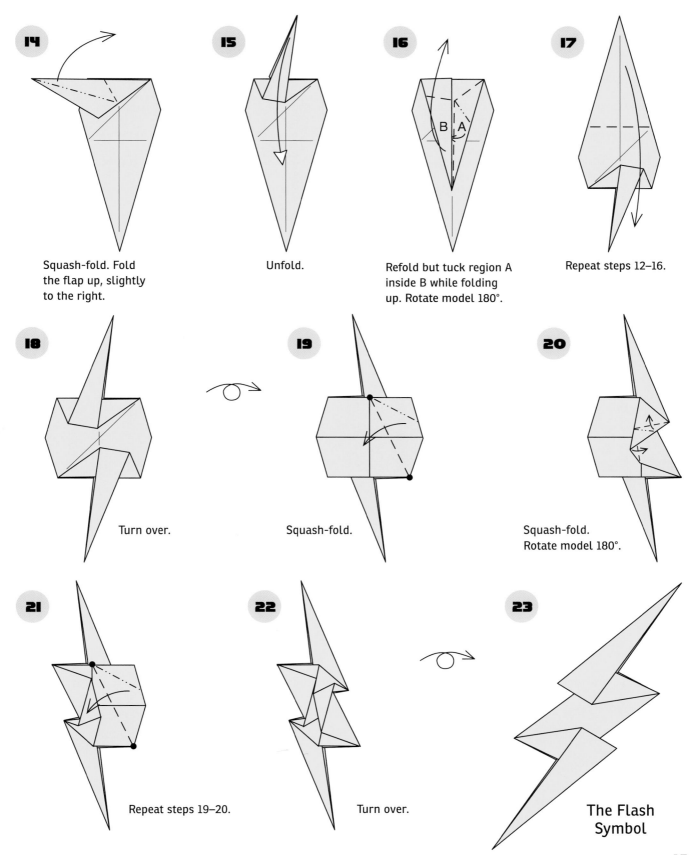

14 Squash-fold. Fold the flap up, slightly to the right.

15 Unfold.

16 Refold but tuck region A inside B while folding up. Rotate model 180°.

17 Repeat steps 12–16.

18 Turn over.

19 Squash-fold.

20 Squash-fold. Rotate model 180°.

21 Repeat steps 19–20.

22 Turn over.

23 The Flash Symbol

GREEN LANTERN SYMBOL

Long ago, an alien race known as the Guardians of the Universe divided space into 3,600 sectors. To protect each of these sectors, they created the Green Lantern Corps. This intergalactic police force's symbol and its color represent willpower. With special power rings, Green Lanterns harness willpower to create anything imaginable and guard the galaxy against evil. Thousands of Green Lanterns protect the many sectors of space, but one sacred oath unites them: "In brightest day, in blackest night, no evil shall escape my sight. Let those who worship evil's might, beware my power … Green Lantern's light!"

LEVEL: ★ ☆ ☆

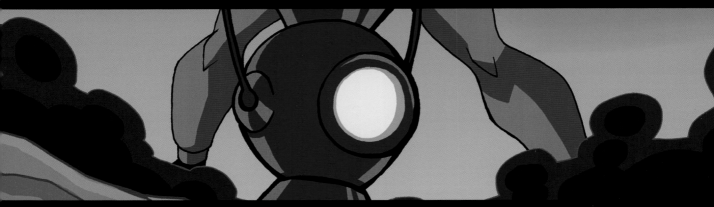

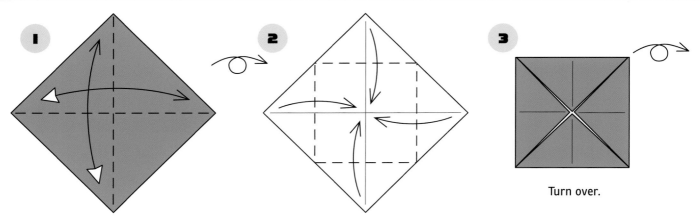

1

Fold and unfold.
Turn over.

2

Fold to the center.

3

Turn over.

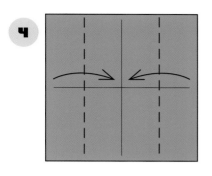

Fold to the center.

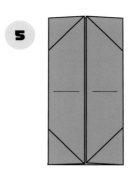

Turn over.

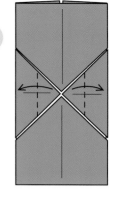

Fold the top layers.

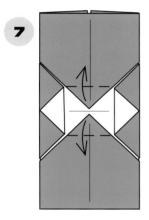

Fold the top layers.

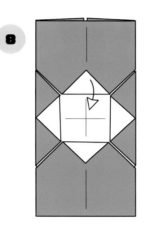

Unfold.

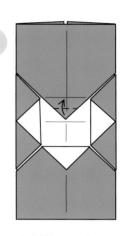

Fold the top layer.

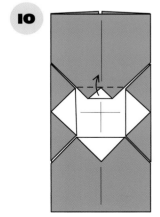

Fold along
the crease.

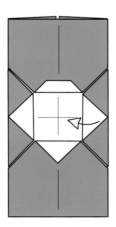

Repeat steps
8–10 three times.

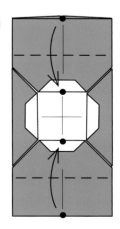

The dots will meet.

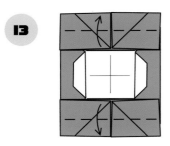

Fold to the top
and bottom.

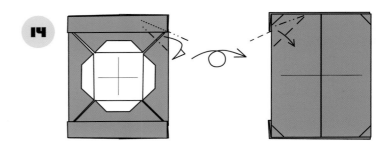

Squash-fold. Turn over
to view the back.

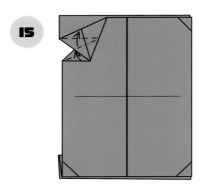

Squash-fold.

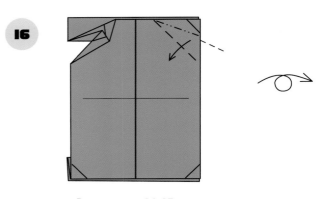

Repeat steps 14–15
three times. Turn over.

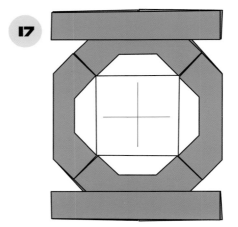

Green Lantern
Symbol

GREEN LANTERN B'DG

Members of the Green Lantern Corps come in all shapes, sizes, and species—including space squirrels! B'dg (pronounced like "badge") may look small, but he is a full-fledged Green Lantern. He guards Space Sector 1014, which includes his home planet, H'lven. Like all Green Lanterns, B'dg wears a power ring, which is fueled by his own willpower. With the ring, B'dg can fly, create anything imaginable, and protect his sector of space.

LEVEL: ★★☆

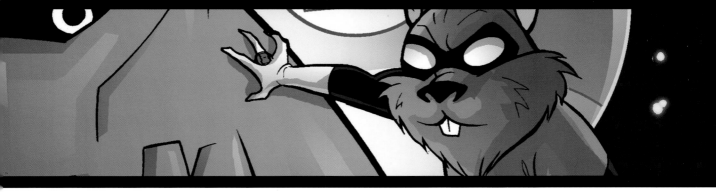

 1

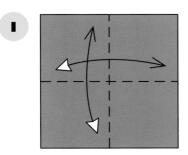

Fold and unfold.
Turn over.

2

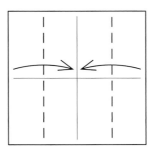

Fold to the center.

3

Fold and unfold.

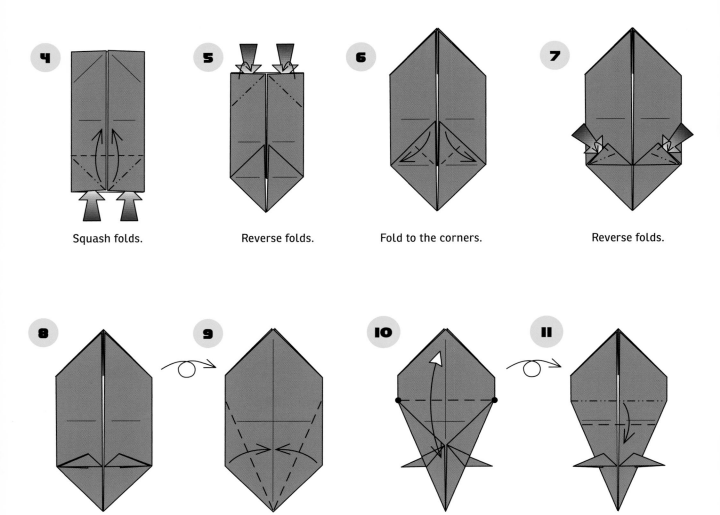

4 Squash folds.

5 Reverse folds.

6 Fold to the corners.

7 Reverse folds.

8 Turn over.

9 Fold to the center.

10 Fold and unfold. Turn over.

11 Pleat-fold. Valley-fold slightly below the crease.

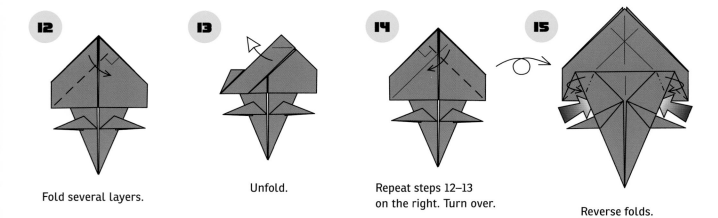

12 Fold several layers.

13 Unfold.

14 Repeat steps 12–13 on the right. Turn over.

15 Reverse folds.

16

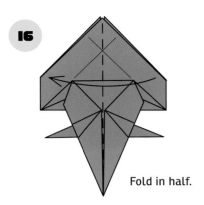

Fold in half.

17

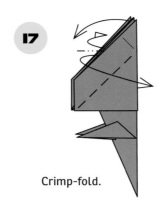

Crimp-fold.

18

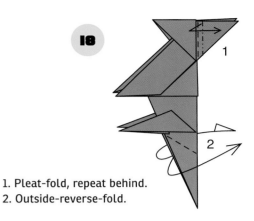

1. Pleat-fold, repeat behind.
2. Outside-reverse-fold.

19

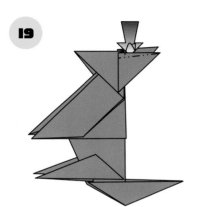

Make a small reverse fold on the left side of the ear. Repeat behind and rotate model.

20

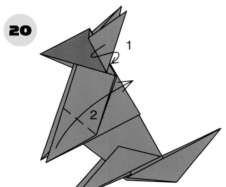

1. Tuck the ear under the darker paper.
2. Fold the arm. Repeat behind.

21

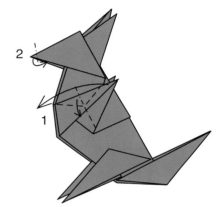

1. Rabbit-ear, repeat behind.
2. Reverse-fold.

22

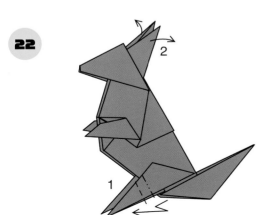

1. Crimp-fold, repeat behind.
2. Spread the ears.

23

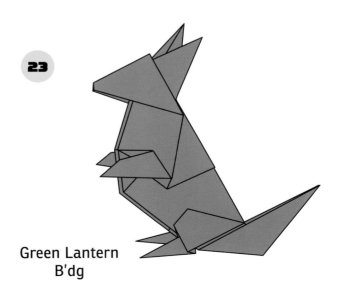

Green Lantern B'dg

GREEN LANTERN HAL JORDAN

Hal Jordan was a brash and reckless test pilot for Ferris Aircraft. One day he discovered the severely injured alien Abin Sur in a crashed spaceship. Before he died, Abin Sur gave Hal his Green Lantern power ring. Now Hal guards Space Sector 2814, which includes the planet Earth. As a former test pilot, he is no stranger to overcoming fear, an essential trait of any member of the Green Lantern Corps. On Hal's finger, the Green Lantern power ring becomes an unmatched weapon—a powerful force to shield his home planet against evil.

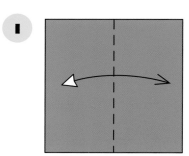

LEVEL: ★ ★ ★

1

Fold and unfold.
Turn over.

2

Fold and unfold.

3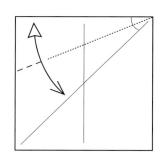

Fold to the crease and unfold. Crease on the left.

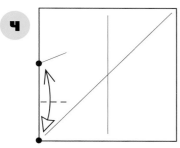

4 Fold and unfold on the left so the dots meet.

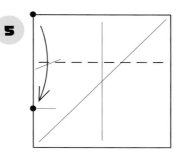

5 Fold down so the dots meet.

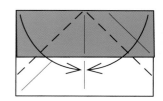

6 Fold to the center.

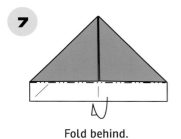

7 Fold behind.

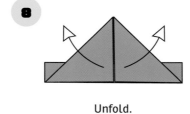

8 Unfold.

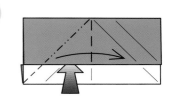

9 Squash-fold.

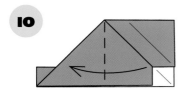

10 Fold the top flap.

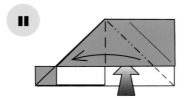

11 Repeat steps 9–10 on the right.

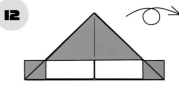

12 Turn over.

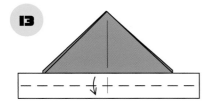

13 Fold down.

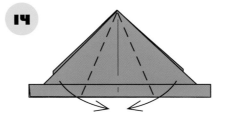

14 Fold to the center.

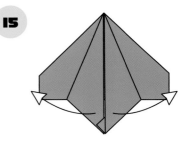

15 Unfold.

16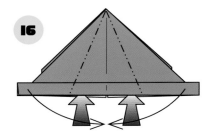

Reverse folds.

17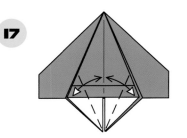

Fold and unfold the top flaps to the center.

18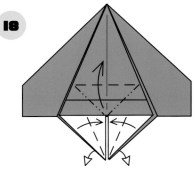

Petal-fold. Spread at the bottom.

19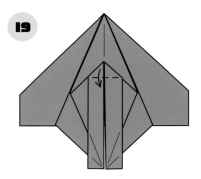

Fold down.

20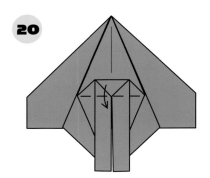

Fold down.

21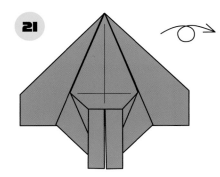

Turn over.

22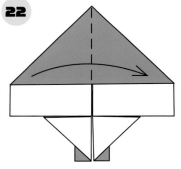

Fold to the right.

23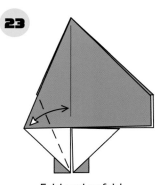

Fold and unfold.

24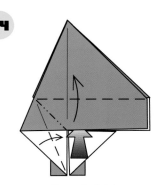

Squash-fold.

25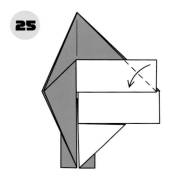

Fold down.

26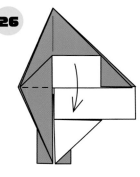

Fold down.

27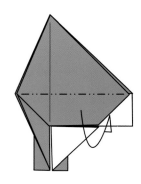

Fold inside.

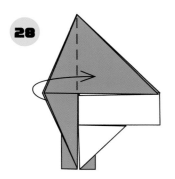

Fold the top flap
to the right.

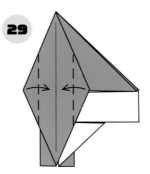

Fold near the center.

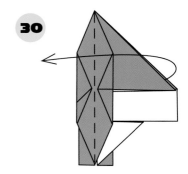

Fold to the left.

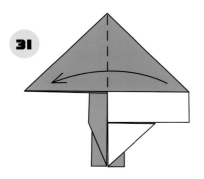

Repeat steps 22–30 in
the opposite direction.

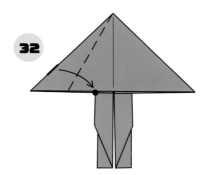

Bring the left
edge to the dot.

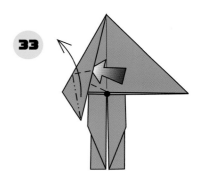

Squash-fold.

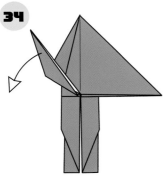

Unfold.

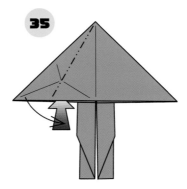

Reverse-fold
along the crease.

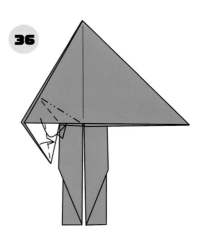

Fold inside along the
creases. Repeat behind.

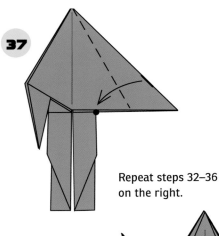

37

Repeat steps 32–36 on the right.

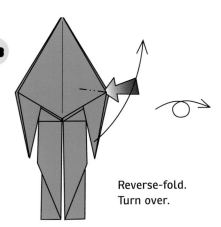

38

Reverse-fold.
Turn over.

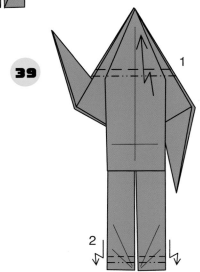

39

1. Pleat-fold the head.
2. Pleat-fold the feet.

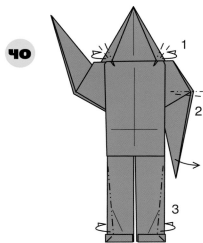

40

1. Shape the neck with small squash folds.
2. Crimp-fold the arm.
3. Squash-fold to shape the feet and legs.

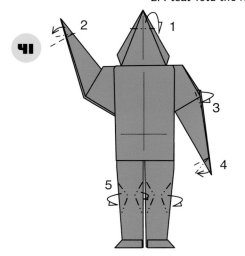

41

1. Fold behind.
2. Squash-fold.
3. Fold inside, repeat behind.
4. Squash-fold.
5. Shape the legs to make them 3D.

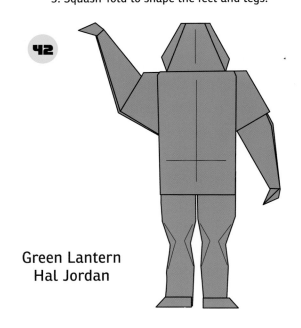

42

Green Lantern
Hal Jordan

26

STORM

As Aquaman's mighty steed, Storm helps protect the Seven Seas, including the royal city of Atlantis. With telepathic powers and tsunami-like speed, Storm is no ordinary sea horse. He carries the Sea King into battle against natural disasters and underwater enemies such as Black Manta and Ocean Master. Together, Aquaman and Storm ensure that Atlantis—and all of the wonders it contains—is never lost again.

LEVEL: ★★☆

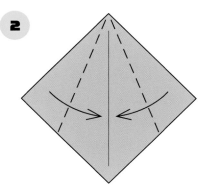

1

Fold and unfold.

2

Fold to the center.

3

Turn over.

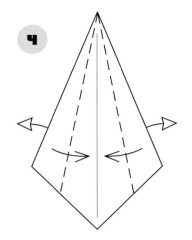

4

Fold to the center and swing out from behind.

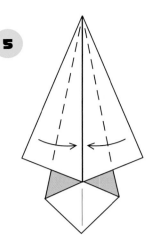

5

Fold to the center.

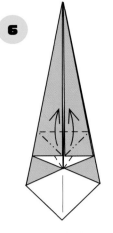

6

Squash folds.

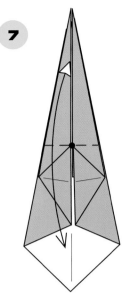

7

Fold and unfold.

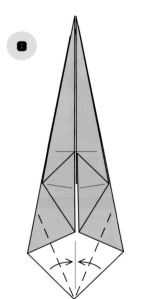

8

Fold to the center.

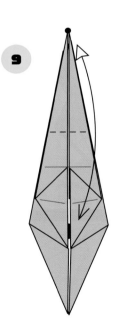

9

Fold and unfold. Bring the dot to the bold line. There is no exact landmark.

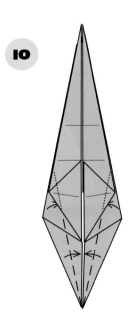

10

Fold to the center and tuck under the top layer.

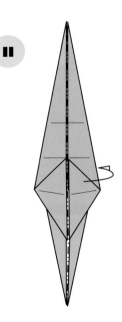

11

Fold in half.

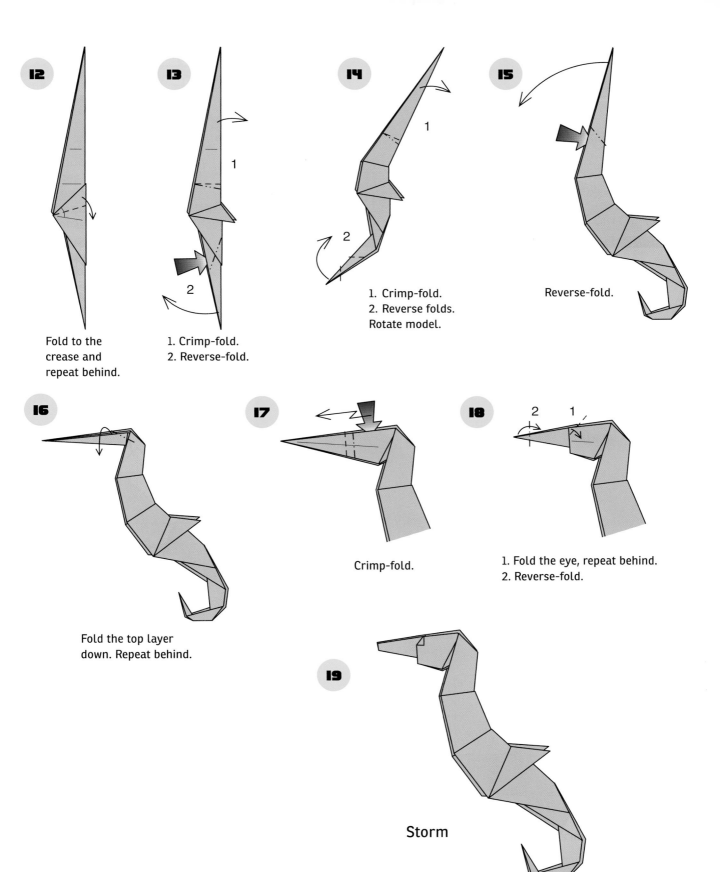

12

Fold to the
crease and
repeat behind.

13

1

2

1. Crimp-fold.
2. Reverse-fold.

14

1

2

1. Crimp-fold.
2. Reverse folds.
Rotate model.

15

Reverse-fold.

16

Fold the top layer
down. Repeat behind.

17

Crimp-fold.

18

2   1

1. Fold the eye, repeat behind.
2. Reverse-fold.

19

Storm

AQUAMAN'S TRIDENT

The trident is a centuries-old symbol for Neptune, the ancient Roman god of the sea. The trident was known as "Earthshaker" because Neptune could create shattering earthquakes by striking it into coastlines or seabeds. As the new oceanic ruler, Aquaman now wields the golden trident and uses it to command the seven seas. The mighty three-pronged weapon can defeat his foes by emitting force fields, creating giant columns of water, or generating whirlpools and turbulent tidal waves.

LEVEL: ★ ★ ☆

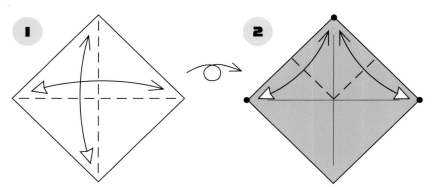

1 Fold and unfold. Turn over.

2 Fold and unfold on the upper half.

3 Bring the bottom corner to the line. Crease on the right.

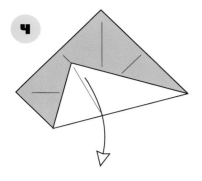

4

Unfold.

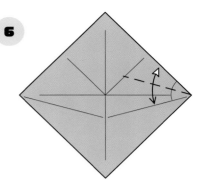

5

Repeat steps 3–4 in
the opposite direction.

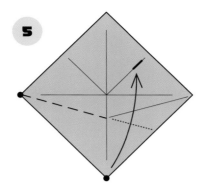

6

Fold and unfold.

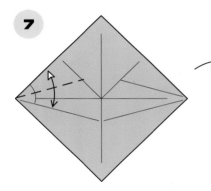

7

Fold and unfold.
Turn over.

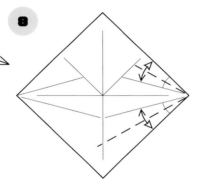

8

Fold and unfold.

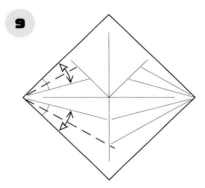

9

Fold and unfold.

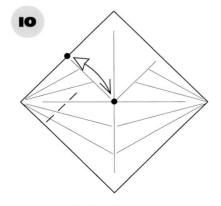

10

Fold and unfold
on the left.

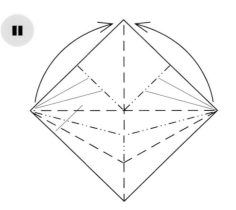

11

Fold along the
creases and flatten.

12

Reverse-fold,
repeat behind.

31

13

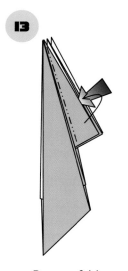

Reverse-fold,
repeat behind.

14

Fold in half.

15

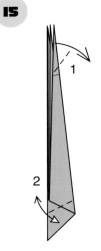

1 Outside-reverse-fold
   slightly above the crease.
2. Fold and unfold.

16

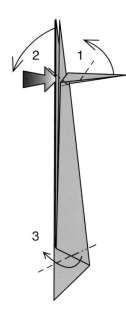

1. Outside-reverse-fold.
2. Reverse-fold.
3. Reverse-fold.

17

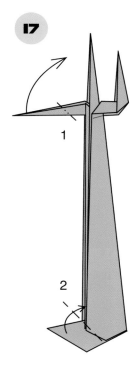

1. Reverse-fold.
2. Fold inside.

18

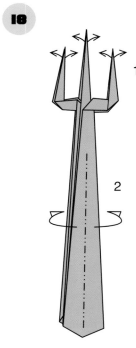

1. Spread the tips.
2. Thin.

19

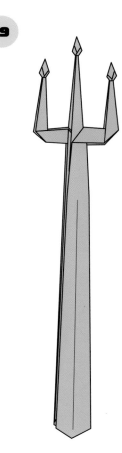

Aquaman's
Trident

AQUAMAN

As the King of the Seven Seas, Aquaman defends all living things that call the ocean home. His telepathic powers enable him to communicate with all sea creatures, from shrimp and whales to hammerhead sharks and electric eels. Obeying their ruler's commands, these ocean dwellers pursue evildoers who treat the ocean as their private treasure trove, or use it as their hideout. Just as Superman and Batman fight for justice above the waves, Aquaman ensures that the two-thirds of our planet below the waves are washed clean of crime.

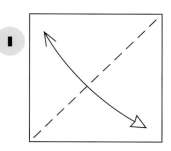

1. Fold and unfold.

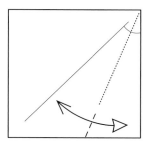

2. Fold to the center and unfold. Crease at the bottom.

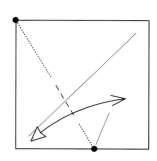

3. Fold and unfold on the diagonal.

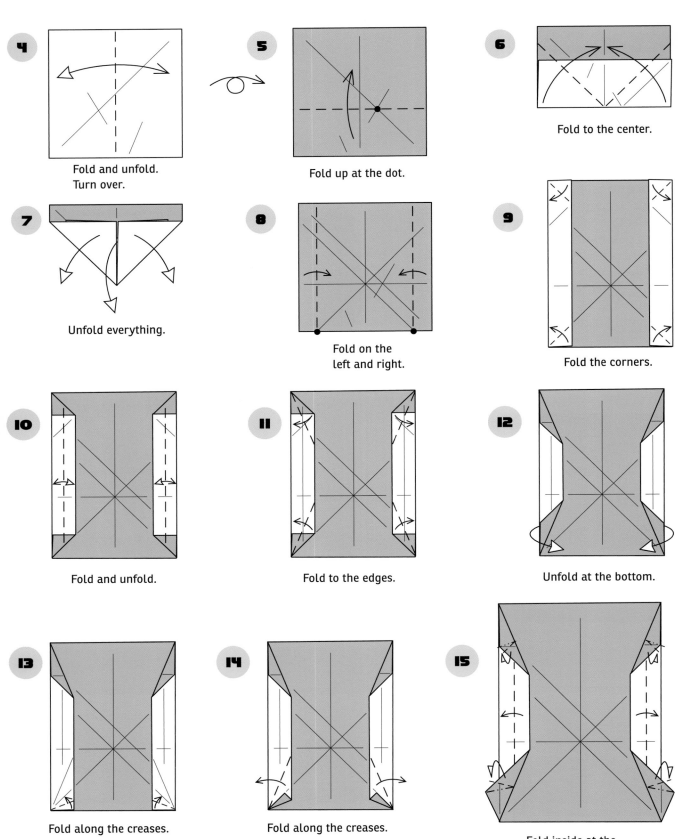

4 Fold and unfold. Turn over.

5 Fold up at the dot.

6 Fold to the center.

7 Unfold everything.

8 Fold on the left and right.

9 Fold the corners.

10 Fold and unfold.

11 Fold to the edges.

12 Unfold at the bottom.

13 Fold along the creases.

14 Fold along the creases.

15 Fold inside at the top and bottom.

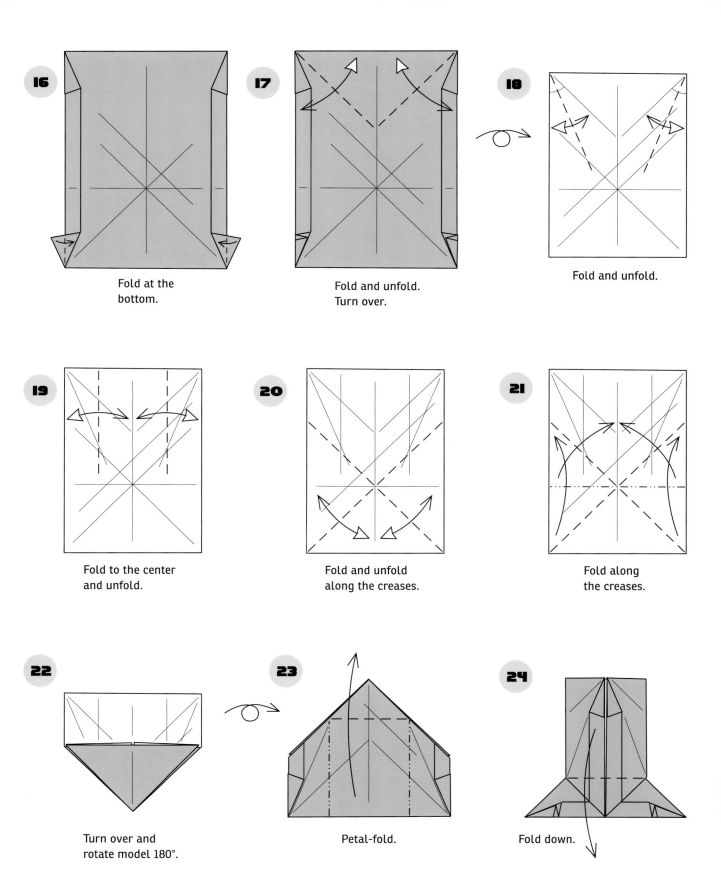

16 Fold at the bottom.

17 Fold and unfold. Turn over.

18 Fold and unfold.

19 Fold to the center and unfold.

20 Fold and unfold along the creases.

21 Fold along the creases.

22 Turn over and rotate model 180°.

23 Petal-fold.

24 Fold down.

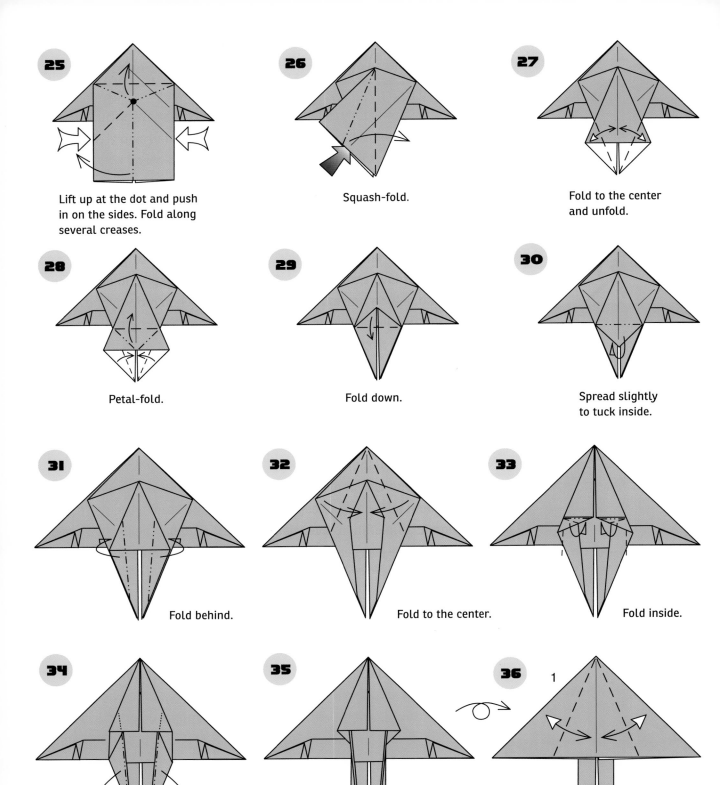

25 Lift up at the dot and push in on the sides. Fold along several creases.

26 Squash-fold.

27 Fold to the center and unfold.

28 Petal-fold.

29 Fold down.

30 Spread slightly to tuck inside.

31 Fold behind.

32 Fold to the center.

33 Fold inside.

34 Fold inside.

35 Turn over.

36
1
2
1. Fold to the center and unfold.
2. Make small squash folds.

37

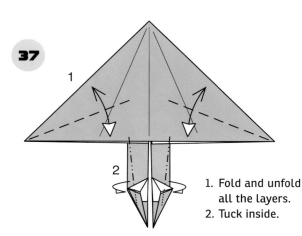

1. Fold and unfold all the layers.
2. Tuck inside.

38

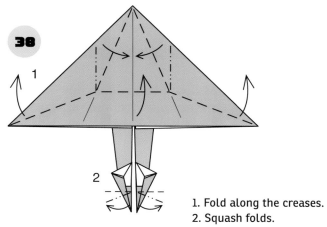

1. Fold along the creases.
2. Squash folds.

39

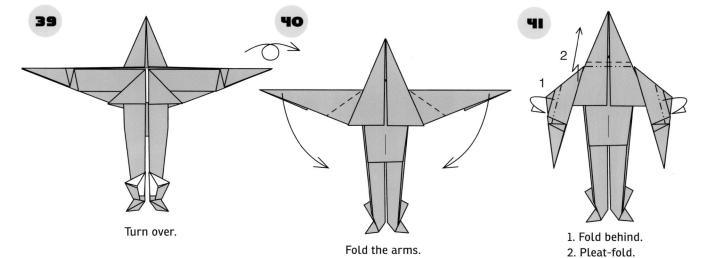

Turn over.

40

Fold the arms.

41

1. Fold behind.
2. Pleat-fold.

42

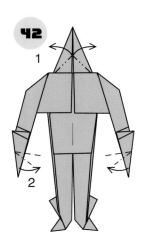

1. Spread.
2. Squash folds.

43

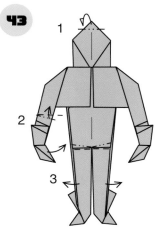

1. Fold behind.
2. Pleat-fold.
3. Pleat folds.

44

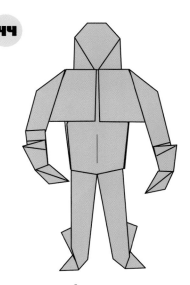

Aquaman

HAWKGIRL

Hawkgirl swoops down on evildoers in Midway City. As a law enforcer from the distant planet Thanagar, she came to Earth to enhance her crime-fighting skills. By working undercover at the Midway City Museum, Hawkgirl remains ready to soar. When duty calls, she straps on her wing-harness and cowl, snatches an ancient weapon from the museum's collection, and takes flight as a feathered figure of swift justice.

LEVEL: ★★★

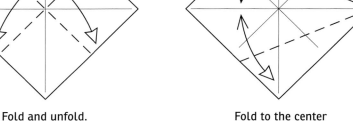

1

Fold and unfold. Turn over.

2

Fold and unfold.

3

Fold to the center and unfold.

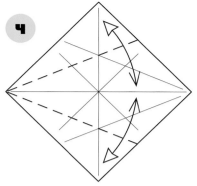

4

Fold to the center and unfold.

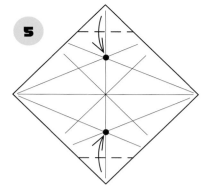

5

Fold to the dots.

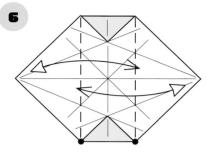

6

Fold and unfold.

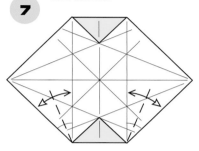

7

Fold and unfold on the left and right.

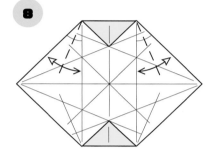

8

Fold and unfold on the left and right.

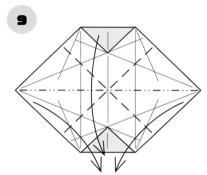

9

Fold along the creases. This is similar to the preliminary fold.

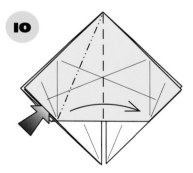

10

Squash-fold.

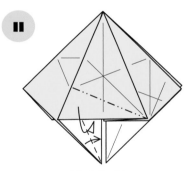

11

Tuck inside.

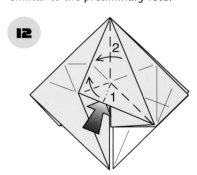

12

Lift up at 1 while folding to the left at 2.

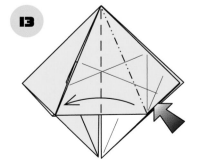

13

Repeat steps 10–12 on the right.

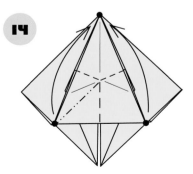

14

This is similar to a rabbit-ear. The dots will meet at the top.

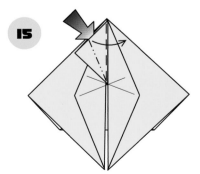

15

Squash–fold.

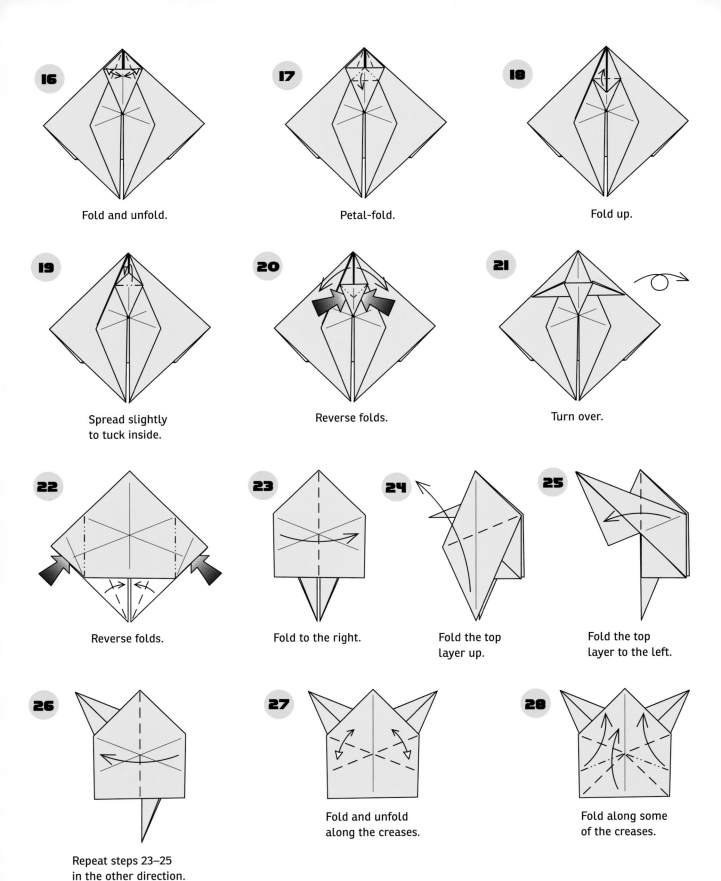

16 Fold and unfold.

17 Petal-fold.

18 Fold up.

19 Spread slightly to tuck inside.

20 Reverse folds.

21 Turn over.

22 Reverse folds.

23 Fold to the right.

24 Fold the top layer up.

25 Fold the top layer to the left.

26 Repeat steps 23–25 in the other direction.

27 Fold and unfold along the creases.

28 Fold along some of the creases.

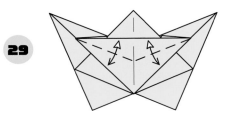

29

Fold and unfold
the top flap.

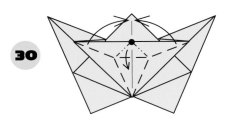

30

Fold the dot down while
bringing the other flaps
to the center.

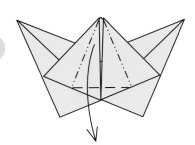

31

Petal-fold. Mountain-fold
along the creases.

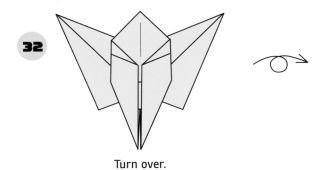

32

Turn over.

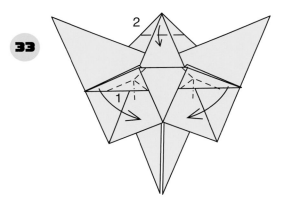

33

1. Rabbit-ear the arms.
2. Fold down.

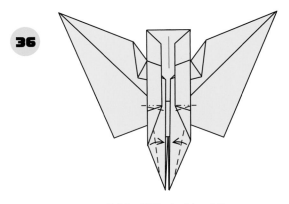

34

Reverse folds. Turn over.

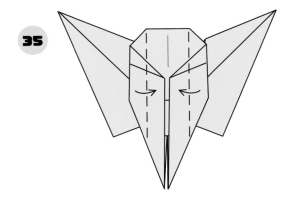

35

Fold toward the center.

36

Fold a little inside at the
top to thin the legs.

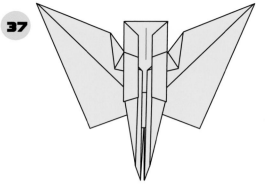

37

Turn over.

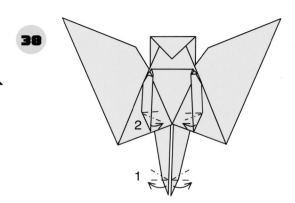

38

1. Crimp-fold the feet.
2. Squash-fold the hands.

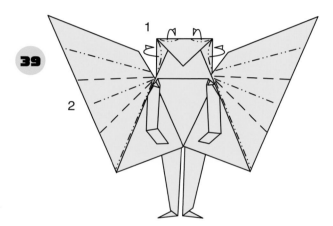

39

1. Shape the head.
2. Pleat-fold the wings.

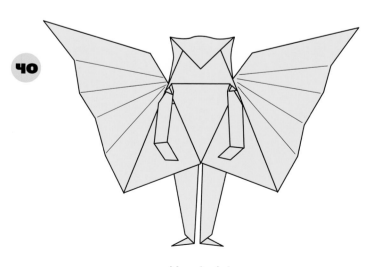

40

Hawkgirl

THE ATOM

Scientist Ray Palmer used the elements from a fallen dwarf star to create a daring device that alters his size from man to microbe. As The Atom he surfs the digital waves between phones, slips through the electrons of locked doors, and hitches rides in criminals' coat collars. Although the Mighty Mite may be a mere six inches tall, he packs a full-size punch by retaining the density and strength of his normal human height. Whether halting a jewel heist or saving the planet from peril, the world's smallest super hero banks on his tiny stature and huge brainpower to cut evil down to size.

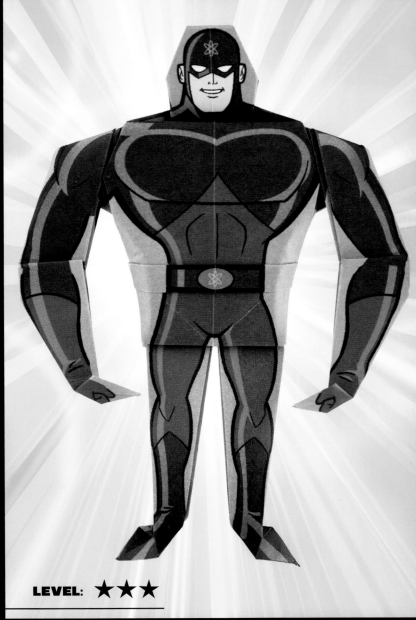

LEVEL: ★★★

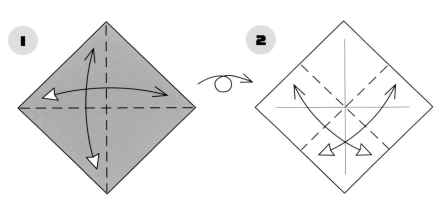

1

Fold and unfold.
Turn over.

2

Fold and unfold.

3

Fold to the center
and unfold.

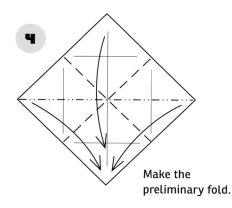

4

Make the preliminary fold.

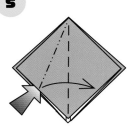

5

Squash-fold. Repeat behind.

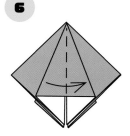

6

Fold the top layer. Repeat behind.

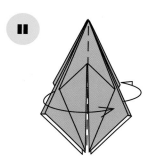

7

Squash-fold. Repeat behind.

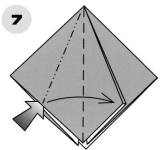

8

Fold to the center. Repeat behind.

9

Unfold. Repeat behind.

10

Petal-fold. Repeat behind.

11

Fold two layers to the right. Repeat behind.

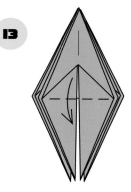

12

Petal-fold. Repeat behind.

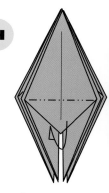

13

Fold down.

14

Spread slightly to fold inside.

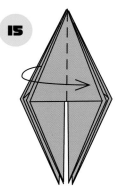

15

Fold two flaps to the left.

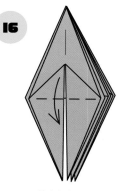

16

Fold down.

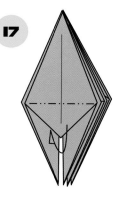

17

Spread slightly to fold inside.

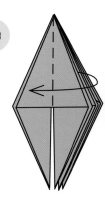

18

Fold two flaps to the right.

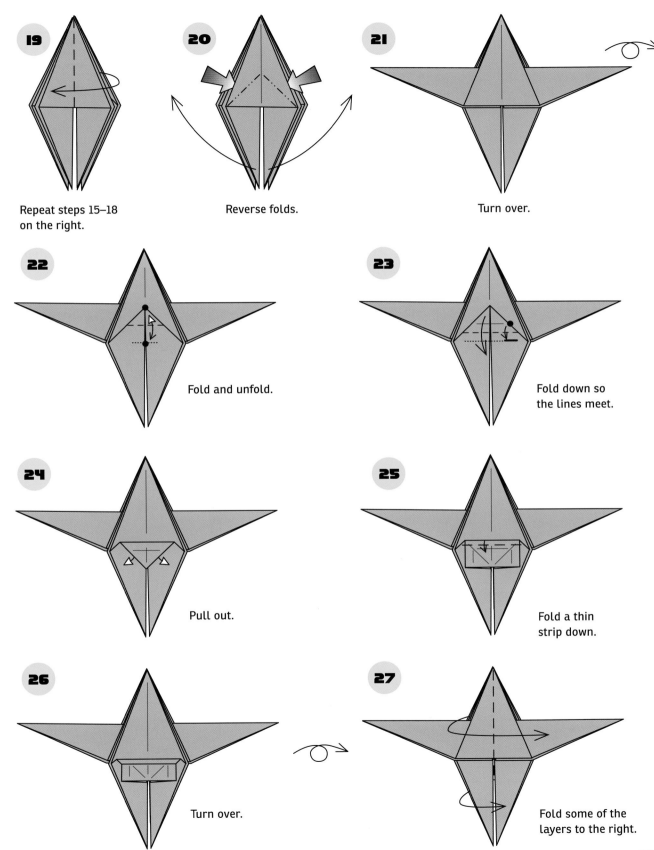

19

Repeat steps 15–18 on the right.

20

Reverse folds.

21

Turn over.

22

Fold and unfold.

23

Fold down so the lines meet.

24

Pull out.

25

Fold a thin strip down.

26

Turn over.

27

Fold some of the layers to the right.

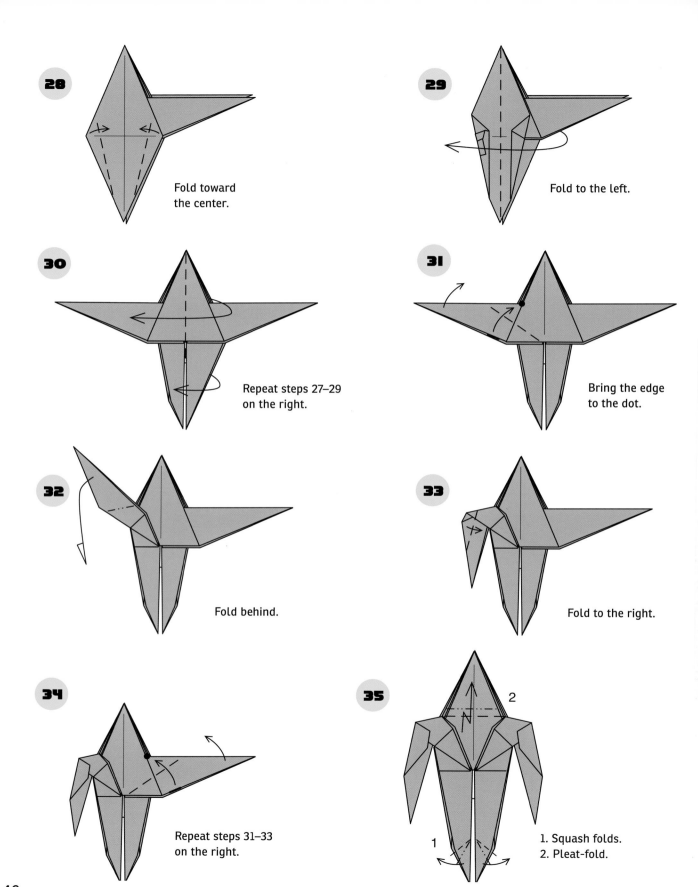

28 Fold toward the center.

29 Fold to the left.

30 Repeat steps 27–29 on the right.

31 Bring the edge to the dot.

32 Fold behind.

33 Fold to the right.

34 Repeat steps 31–33 on the right.

35
1. Squash folds.
2. Pleat-fold.

36

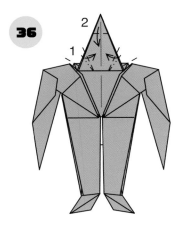

1. Squash folds.
2. Fold down.

37

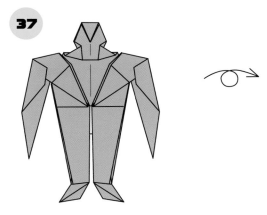

Turn over.

38

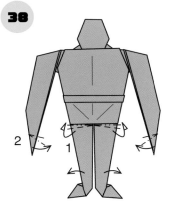

1. Pleat-fold the legs.
2. Squash-fold the hands.

39

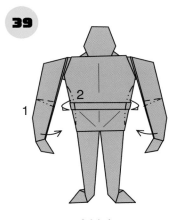

1. Pleat-fold the arms.
2. Shape the body.

40

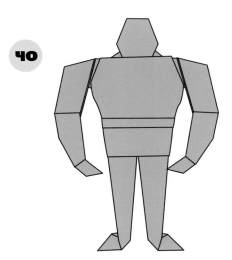

The Atom

Read More

Harbo, Christopher. *Origami Folding Frenzy: Boats, Fish, Cranes, and More!* Origami Paperpalooza. North Mankato, Minn.: Capstone Press, 2015.

Montroll, John. *Batman Origami: Amazing Folding Projects Featuring the Dark Knight.* DC Origami. North Mankato, Minn.: Capstone Press, 2015.

Montroll, John. *Dragons and Other Fantastic Creatures in Origami.* New York: Dover Publications, 2014.

Robinson, Nick. *World's Best Origami.* New York: Alpha, 2010.

Internet Sites

FactHound offers a safe, fun way to find Internet sites related to this book. All of the sites on FactHound have been researched by our staff.

Here's all you do:

Visit *www.facthound.com*

Type in this code: 9781491417898

Super-cool stuff! Check out projects, games and lots more at www.capstonekids.com

ABOUT THE AUTHOR

John Montroll is respected for his work in origami throughout the world. His published work has significantly increased the global repertoire of original designs in origami. John is also acknowledged for developing new techniques and groundbreaking bases. The American origami master is known for being the inspiration behind the single-square, no cuts, no glue approach in origami.

John started folding in elementary school. He quickly progressed from folding models from books to creating his own designs. John has written many books, and each model that he designs has a meticulously developed folding sequence. John's long-standing experience allows him to accomplish a model in fewer steps rather than more. It is his constant endeavor to give the reader a pleasing folding experience.